Mark O'Brien O'Reilly is a leading barrister with a growing reputation for experience and skill beyond his call. He is ranked as one of the top junior planning barristers in the country by Planning Magazine's Planning Law Survey 2024 (and also holds a ranking as one of the top ten planning barristers under the age of 35 with Planning Magazine noting his particular injunction expertise). The High Court has described his submissions as "concise and well-structured". Clients have praised him as "commercial" and "user friendly". Mark regularly appears at planning inquiries concerning a broad range of developments. He also has a busy High Court practice and is regularly called upon, often urgently, to advise upon and obtain High Court planning injunctions (and has acted in many of the recent reported cases concerning section 187B injunctions). He has a broad range of clients ranging from developers, renewable energy companies and landowners to local residents. He has extensive experience of acting for, and advising, central government and local government (and has acted for many London boroughs). He is a First-Class Honours graduate of University College Dublin (BCL Law with History) and the University of Cambridge (LLM). Mark was called to the Bar of Ireland in July 2023.

A Practical Guide to Injunctions Pursuant to Section 187B of the Town and Country Planning Act 1990

A Practical Guide to Injunctions Pursuant to Section 187B of the Town and Country Planning Act 1990

Mark O'Brien O'Reilly

BCL (NUI), PGDip, LLM (Cantab), BL (King's Inn)

Law Brief Publishing

Published 2025 by Law Brief Publishing, an imprint of Law Brief Publishing Ltd
30 The Parks
Minehead
Somerset
TA24 8BT

www.lawbriefpublishing.com

Paperback: 978-1-916698-71-0

To my mother, Noeline O'Brien, who thought us not only the value of education but provided a fine example of resilience and fortitude. Thank you also to those at the University College Dublin Sutherland School of Law and Queens' College, Cambridge, academics and friends alike, whose teaching and friendship I will aways treasure. To those at Gray's Inn and Francis Taylor Building who have encouraged and supported me in my chosen profession, thank you.

CONTENTS

CHAPTER ONE

INTRODUCTION

The remedy of an injunction has a long history in the laws of England and Wales. It first emerged as an equitable remedy as a flexible invention of the medieval Court of Chancery. It is, of course, a powerful remedy as it is an order of the Court which can either restrain a person or body from doing something ("**a Restraining Injunction**") and/or compel them to do something ("**a Mandatory Injunction**"). As it is an order of the Court, a failure to abide by, or to comply with, the requirements of an injunction is a serious matter. It gives rise to contempt of court and, therefore, as a result the potential for an application for committal in response to that contempt which can result in imprisonment. The threat of that sanction means that, in comparison to some of the other enforcement options open to local planning authorities, it has a unique effect which is bound to focus the minds of even the most intransigent of individuals and entities. Of course, coupled with this is the fact that the Court will want to be satisfied that the circumstances are such to warrant the grant of the unique and powerful remedy that is a planning injunction.

The history of an express statutory power to seek a planning injunction is not a long one. The statutory power which grants Local Planning Authorities ("**LPAs**") the power to ask the Court to make an injunction is section 187B of the Town and Country Planning Act 1990 ("**the 1990 Act**"). Section 187B(1) of the 1990 Act states that "Where a local planning authority consider it necessary or expedient for any actual or apprehended breach of planning control to be restrained by injunction, they may apply to the court for an injunction, whether or not they have exercised or are proposing to exercise any of their other powers under this Part". That power was introduced into the 1990 Act by virtue of the Planning and Compensation Act 1991. That itself came about as a result of a recommendation made by Robert Carnwarth QC (as he then was, later Lord Carnwarth of the Supreme Court) in his seminal 1989 report *Enforcing Planning Control.*

That is not to say that LPAs could not seek an injunction from the Court in suitable cases prior to the enactment of section 187B of the 1990 Act. LPAs could do so by reference to, for example, the Local Government Act 1972 or by asking to the Court to rely on its equitable power to grant an injunction in an appropriate case. The recommendation of the Carnwarth report was, however, that the circumstances in which such an injunction could be sought and granted should be formally set out within the statute. In particular, the Carnwarth report was keen that a statutory recognition ought to be given to what was considered by the author to be a "useful weapon in the planning armoury" (paragraph 2.23). The recommendation of the report was, therefore, that LPAs should be empowered to ask the Court to grant an injunction where there was an actual or apprehended breach of planning control. The author envisaged that there would be two particular sets of circumstances in which it would be a useful tool: to "provide an urgent remedy in cases where there is a serious threat to amenity"; and to "provide a stronger back-up power in cases where the existing remedies have proved, or are thought likely to be, inadequate" (paragraph 10.2). The report was clear, however, that it would "a mistake to attempt to prescribe too closely the circumstances in which the remedy would be available" as experience had shown that "the merit of the remedy is its flexibility and its ability to evolve to meet changing needs". That recommendation was accepted by government and amongst the fruits of the labour of the Carnwarth report was the insertion of section 187B into the 1990 Act.

It is of note, however, that the statutory power to seek an injunction is strictly limited to the LPA. That can be contrasted with, for example, the analogous provision in Irish planning law which is section 160 of the Planning and Development Act 2000. It grants a power "Where an unauthorised development has been, is being or is likely to be carried out or continued" to "a planning authority or any other person, whether or not the person has an interest in the land" to seek an injunction. That might be one such reform which could be made here in the UK. Of course, although the benefits seem numerous, e.g. removing pressure on under resourced LPAs and/or allowing local residents to seek an injunction where the LPA has resolved not to act, etc, one can also see the potential for unmeritorious, vexatious or purely tactical applications to be made. Nevertheless, the Irish experience might offer fruit for thought to any Secretary of State who thought it was time to expand the scope of section 187B of the 1990 Act.

It has indeed proven to be a versatile remedy. The circumstances in which an injunction might be sought or granted are infinite. Perhaps of the most common scenarios is where an unauthorised encampment has been created on land without planning permission by, for example, gypsies or travellers or travelling showpeople. But that is not the only situation in which an injunction might be sought. It could, for example, be used by a LPA to require a developer to comply with conditions relating to, for example, highways safety or public open space before selling or allow the occupation of units within a development. It might be sought where, for example, unauthorised commercial activity is having a detrimental impact on residential amenity or on highways safety. And the applications made by several LPAs to seek to retrain the use of hotels as hostels for temporary asylum seeker accommodation as part of arrangements made by the Home Secretary show the potential for the remedy to be relied upon in any infinite number of situations (see, for example, *Fenland District Council v CBPRP Limited* [2022] EWHC 3132 (KB). What lies behind each and every case, however, is the need for the Court, in determining an application, to strike the balance between public and private interests.

The aim of this book is to provide a practical guide to the law in this area. It will address, for example, the law setting out the principles to be applied when the Court is determining an application. It will also address practical matters such as the procedural requirements for an application. It will be of use not only to practitioners in this area but also to LPAs and developers alike as the book will also consider how to respond to such an application. It aims to be the go-to guide for all those involved in the planning and development world who may find themselves either seeking an injunction from the Court or in seeking to defend such an application. The law is believed to be correct and up to date as of the time of writing which is 2 January 2025.

CHAPTER TWO

PLANNING CONTROL AND ENFORCEMENT

In considering the power to seek a planning injunction, it is important to first understand the scope of planning control and how a breach of planning control might arise. An important first step for the LPA is to identify whether there is an actual or apprehended breach of planning control. It will also need to consider, of course, whether any other enforcement action might be more suitable in determining whether it is "necessary and expedient" to seek an injunction.

The House of Lords, in what is the leading case for this area of planning law, *South Buckinghamshire DC v Porter* [2003] 2 A.C. 558 ("***South Bucks***"), said that "What uses should or should not be allowed of lands within the area of the authority, what developments should or should not be permitted to take place upon such lands, are questions for the planning authorities and not for courts of law to resolve" (paragraph 67). The House of Lords endorsed the judgment of Simon Brown LJ in the Court of Appeal where he said that "It seems to me perfectly clear that the judge on a section 187B application is not required, nor even entitled, to reach his own independent view of the planning merits of the case. These he is required to take as decided within the planning process, the actual or anticipated breach of planning control being given when he comes to exercise his discretion" (paragraph 53).

It might be thought, therefore, that it is not for the Court to determine, as a first step, whether or not there is an actual or apprehend breach of planning control. That has not, however, been the way in which the Courts have approached most applications before it for a planning injunction. That seems obvious. An injunction is a serious remedy, and the High Court will need to be persuaded that there is an actual or apprehended breach of planning control which entitles the LPA to rely on the statutory power. That approach was endorsed in the obiter comments of the High Court in *Durham County Council v Secretary of State for Levelling Up, Housing and Communities* [2023] EWHC 1394 (Admin) where the Court said that "Neither Simon Brown LJ nor Lord Bingham was saying that the court could not or should not decide the threshold question whether the development was an actual or apprehended breach of planning control, if there was a dispute about that. If, for example, it was the respondent's case that what he was proposing to do did not require planning permission, the court could not avoid reaching its own view about that" (paragraph 34). The LPA will need, therefore, to set out in its evidence how it says that the answer to that threshold question is yes. How much consideration that question requires at the hearing will depend on what the Defendant's position is. The Defendant may simply accept that there has been a breach but equally, in some cases, it may argue that the development is not a breach of planning control, e.g. because a change of use is not material in planning terms or because the development is authorised by an extant planning permission, etc.

Section 57(1) of the 1990 Act provides that "planning permission is required for the carrying out of any development of land". Section 55(1) of the 1990 Act defines "development" as the "carrying out of building, engineering, mining or other operations in, on, over or under land" (**operational development**) or "the making of any material change in the use of any buildings or other land" (**material change of use**). Land, for the purposes of the 1990 Act, is "any corporeal hereditament, including a building" (section 336) – that definition differs from the general definition of land in the Interpretation Act 1978. As to the last point, it was held in *R (Parkes) v Dorset Council* [2024] EWHC 1253 (Admin) that, for the purposes of the 1990 Act, and planning control, land refers "to the solid part of the earth's surface as opposed to the sea" (paragraph 179). This meant that in that case the High Court concluded that the seabed above which the Bibby Stockholm was moored was not land subject to planning control (see paragraph 195).

Operational development will include any groundworks, building alterations, construction works, demolition, the laying of hardstanding and other operations such as mining or engineering operations.

As to whether or not there has been a material change of use (which must be determined by reference to the planning unit (see *Burdle v Secretary of State for the Environment* [1972] 1 WLR 1027 for assistance in identifying the correct planning unit)), this will be a question of fact and degree. In determining that question, it will be important to consider if there has been a change in the character of the use (see *Manchester City Council v Secretary of State for Housing, Communities and Local Government* [2021] EWCA Civ 1920, [16]). The answer will always depend upon the particular characteristics of the use in question (*Moore v Secretary of State for Communities and Local Government* [2012] EWCA Civ 1202, [27]). Off-site impacts can be relevant to that consideration.

A change of use must be material in planning terms for it to constitute a material change of use. The most obvious example might be the change of use of agricultural land to residential use by placing caravans and mobile homes on the land which are then used for residential occupation. A material change of use can also come about through an intensification in a particular use of land. There can, however, be a change in the use of the land, which is not a material change of use and, therefore, will not be a breach of planning control. The policies of the development plan may be relevant, therefore, to deciding whether there has been a material change of use (see, e.g. *R (Wright) v*

Resilient Energy Severndale Limited [2019] UKSC 53 and *Great Yarmouth Borough Council v Al-Abdin* [2022] EWHC 3476 (KB)). In the latter case, in which an injunction was sought to prevent the use of a hotel as a hostel for asylum seekers, it was said by the High Court that although "At the end of the day whether a material change of use would occur is a question of fact and degree, but in my judgment the particular policy considerations raised in this case by Policy GY6 strengthen the Council's case on breach of planning control significantly" (paragraph 56). The local development plan there had a policy which sought to, inter alia, "resist the loss of key tourism uses to non-tourism uses" (see paragraph 27).

Section 171A of the 1990 Act provides that "carrying out development without the required planning permission" is a breach of planning control. There are, of course, various ways in which planning permission can be granted: following an application to the LPA; on appeal by the Secretary of State; or pursuant to a development order such as the Town and Country Planning (General Permitted Development) (England) Order 2015 ("**Permitted Development**"). The LPA will also need to consider the provisions set out in section 171B of the 1990 Act and ask itself whether the breach is immune from enforcement action. It is unlikely, however, that section 171B will be relevant to many applications for a section 187B injunction as, in most cases, injunctions are sought quickly after the breach has occurred. That may not, however, always be the case. A Defendant may, however, rely on the expiration of a significant degree of time before the application is made (in the absence of recourse to any other enforcement powers) to argue that the LPA's conclusion that an injunction is necessary and expedient is wrong. LPAs should be aware that delay can be relied on by Defendants in seeking to resist the imposition of an injunction. A material change in circumstances might, however, assist the LPA in rebutting that argument.

Section 171A of the 1990 Act also makes clear that it will be a breach of planning control if a developer fails to comply with a condition or limitation attached to any grant of planning permission. An example of the latter breach which might lead to an application for an injunction might be if, for example, a developer had failed to carry out certain works required by a condition to be completed before occupation was allowed but had nevertheless allowed units to be sold and occupied without completing those works. The LPA should be aware, however, that injunctions to enforce breaches of an extant section 106 agreement should be sought pursuant to section 106(5) of the 1990 Act rather than section 187B. Such injunctions raise different considerations outside the scope of this book. It should consider, therefore, whether or not the breach is a breach of planning control or a breach of a section 106 agreement.

The LPA will need to clearly set out in its evidence what is says the breach of planning control is. This will obviously be a more straightforward exercise if an Enforcement Notice has already been issued but LPAs should note that the breach of an Enforcement Notice is not itself a breach of planning control. Further, the LPA should be careful, where an Enforcement Notice has been issued in the past, to consider whether the breach is the same as that which was targeted by the notice or whether the characteristics of the breach have changed in the intervening period in any way.

The LPA will also need to carefully consider, therefore, the planning history and ask itself whether any planning permissions previously granted, whether by the LPA itself or by one of the other routes, in respect of the land authorises the development or whether the development is otherwise Permitted Development. Where the alleged breach of planning control is a material change of use, the evidence will need to clearly set out why the change of use is considered to be material in planning terms. It will also need to identify whether the breach is an "actual", i.e. has already occurred, or an "apprehended" breach, i.e. an anticipatory breach. Of course, in some situations, there may be an actual and an apprehended breach if a certain amount of development has already occurred and further development is anticipated. In other cases, the breach may only be an apprehended breach if, for example, the threatened operational development has not yet been carried out or the material change of use has not yet occurred. The LPA will most often rely, therefore, on a witness statement from a Planning Officer as well as an experienced Enforcement Officer to support its application for an injunction.

Of course, the LPA having identified a breach of planning control, has a number of enforcement options open to it as set out in Part Seven of the 1990 Act. It might, for example, serve a Temporary Stop Notice (section 171E), an Enforcement Notice (section 172), a Stop Notice (section 183) or a Breach of Condition Notice (section 187A). The distinct advantage, however, of a section 187B injunction is that it can be used to target an apprehended breach of planning control whereas the other enforcement powers open to the LPA presuppose an extant breach of planning control. The LPA does not need, therefore, to wait until the breach comes into existence to try and restrain it by way of an injunction. This reflects the historic evolution of the injunction and, in particular, the historic ability to seek an injunction, commonly called a quia timet injunction, where a wrongful act is anticipated. By way of an example, complaints from local residents may indicate that an unauthorised development is about to commence which the LPA considers ought to be restrained by way of an injunction, e.g. a quantity of hardcore has been delivered to a green belt site which indicates that residential occupation is imminent. The LPA does not need to wait until the harmful development has begun to seek an injunction in the way that it would need to wait before, for example, serving an Enforcement Notice, as the power is pre-emptive as it can restrain apprehended breaches as well as extant breaches. It is, therefore, an extremely important tool in the enforcement arsenal.

CHAPTER THREE

THE STATUTORY PROVISIONS

Section 187B of the 1990 Act, in full, reads as follows:

> **Injunctions restraining breaches of planning control**
>
> (1) Where a local planning authority consider it necessary or expedient for any actual or apprehended breach of planning control to be restrained by injunction, they may apply to the court for an injunction, whether or not they have exercised or are proposing to exercise any of their other powers under this Part.
>
> (2) On an application under subsection (1) the court may grant such an injunction as the court thinks appropriate for the purpose of restraining the breach.
>
> (3) Rules of court may provide for such an injunction to be issued against a person whose identity is unknown.
>
> (4) In this section "the court" means the High Court or the county court.

Section 187B of the 1990 Act, confers a statutory power, therefore upon a LPA to seek an injunction in the public interest, i.e. to enforce the system of planning control. It is a statutory jurisdiction and is an established exception, therefore, to the general principle that "an injunction must be founded on an existing cause of action against the persons enjoined" (see paragraph 43 of *Wolverhampton City Council v London Gypsies and Travellers and others* [2023] UKSC 47).

Reference should also be made to section 37(1) of the Senior Courts Act 1981 which provides that "The High Court may by order (whether interlocutory or final) grant an injunction or appoint a receiver in all cases in which it appears to the court to be just and convenient to do so". Section 37(2) (mirroring section 187B(2) of the 1990 Act) further states that "Any such order may be made either unconditionally or on such terms and conditions as the court thinks just". Section 222(1) of the Local Government Act 1972 should also be borne in mind which empowers a local authority to institute civil proceedings where they "consider it expedient for the promotion or protection of the interests of the inhabitants of their area".

CHAPTER FOUR

WHEN MIGHT A PLANNING INJUNCTION BE A SUITABLE REMEDY?

The leading case on the principles which apply to an application for a final section 187B injunction is undoubtedly the aforementioned House of Lords decision in *South Bucks* (although the principles relate to a final injunction, they will also be relevant at the interim injunction stage as discussed later). Holgate J quoted, with approval, at paragraph 93 of *Ipswich*, the principles set out in *South Bucks* as to the grant of permanent injunctions. He summarised as follows the following principles and guidance which emerge from *South Bucks*:

i) The need to enforce planning control in the general interest is a relevant consideration and in that context the planning history of the site may be important. The "degree and flagrancy" of the breach of planning may be critical. Where conventional enforcement measures have failed over a prolonged period the court may be more ready to grant an injunction. The court may be more reluctant where enforcement action has never been taken;

ii) On the other hand, there might be urgency in the situation sufficient to justify the avoidance of an anticipated breach of planning control;

iii) An anticipatory interim injunction may sometimes be preferable to a delayed permanent injunction, for example, where stopping a gypsy moving on to a site in the first place, may involve less hardship than moving him out after a long period of occupation;

iv) While it is not for the court to question the correctness of planning decisions which have been taken (e.g. decisions to refuse a planning permission or to dismiss an appeal), the Court should come to a broad view as to the degree of environmental damage resulting from the breach and the urgency or otherwise of bringing it to an end;

v) The achievement of the legitimate aim of preserving the environment does not always outweigh countervailing rights (or factors). Injunctive relief is unlikely to be granted unless it is a "commensurate" remedy is the circumstances of the case; and

vi) It is the Court's task to strike the balance between competing interests, weighing one against the other.

Holgate J went on to quote, at paragraph 94 of *Ipswich*, the comments of Lord Bingham in *South Bucks* where it was said that "The jurisdiction of the court under section 187B is an original, not a supervisory, jurisdiction" and that "The court's power to grant an injunction under section 187B is a discretionary power. The permissive "may" in subsection (2) applies not only to the terms of any injunction the court may grant but also to the decision whether it should grant any injunction. It is indeed inherent in the concept of an injunction in English law that it is a remedy that the court may but need not grant, depending on its judgment of all the circumstances".

It was also said in *South Bucks* that "The power exists above all to permit abuses to be curbed and urgent solutions provided where these are called for. Since the facts of different cases are infinitely various, no single test can be prescribed to distinguish cases in which the court's discretion should be exercised in favour of granting an injunction from those in which it should not. Where it appears that a breach or apprehended breach will continue or occur unless and until effectively restrained by the law and that nothing short of an injunction will provide effective restraint..., that will point strongly towards the grant of an injunction. So will a history of unsuccessful enforcement and persistent non-compliance, as will evidence that the defendant has played the system by wilfully exploiting every opportunity for prevarication and delay, although section 187B(1) makes plain that a local planning authority, in applying for an injunction, need not have exercised nor propose to exercise any of its other enforcement powers" (paragraph 29).

Holgate J, at paragraph 96 of *Ipswich*, quoted Lord Scott in *South Bucks* who held that "Of particular importance, of course, will be whether or not the local planning authority can establish not only that there is a current or apprehended breach of planning control but also that the ordinary statutory means of enforcement are not likely to be effective in preventing the breach or bringing it to an end. In a case in which the statutory procedure of enforcement notice, prosecution for non-compliance and exercise by the authority of such statutory self-help remedies as are available had not been tried and where there was no sufficient reason to assume that, if tried, they would not succeed in dealing with the breach, the local planning authority would be unlikely to succeed in persuading the court that the grant of an injunction would be just and convenient" (paragraph 99 of *South Bucks*).

The LPA will need, therefore, to set out in its evidence why it considers that an injunction is necessary and why the other statutory methods of enforcement open to it are not likely to be effective. This could be justified in a number of ways, e.g. the likely delays in securing an end to the breach if an appeal is made against an Enforcement Notice as the effect of the 1990 Act is that that the Enforcement

Notice does not take effect until the final determination of any appeal. In *Chelmsford City Council v Lee* [2019] EWHC 756 (QB), the breach of planning control was an unauthorised traveller development consisting of the stationing of caravans on land within the Green Belt and open countryside (paragraph 3). It was said that "The local authority were criticised in the course of the trial for seeking an injunction rather than taking some other form of enforcement such as service of a stop notice or an enforcement notice" (paragraph 33). This criticism was, however, rejected by the High Court who said that "in my judgment, it is entirely understandable why, in light of the information that they had, that the local authority decided that an injunction application made without notice was the appropriate way forward. They had limited knowledge of what the intentions of the defendants were, they had a very real concern, an understandable concern, that if they did not move quickly the land would be further developed and the situation would become worse or more difficult, there would be inherent delays in service of a stop notice or an enforcement notice, with further uncertainty being created and, in my judgment, the local authority cannot properly be criticised for deciding to seek immediate relief through the High Court rather than taking one of those alternative approaches" (paragraph 33).

Of course, where an Enforcement Notice has been served, and taken effect, and has not been complied with, it will be easier for the LPA to show that conventional enforcement methods have failed. In *Epping Forest DC v Halama* [2023] EWHC 2906 (KB), the High Court, at paragraph 43, concluded that, in light of the facts of that case which included the issuance of an Enforcement Notice, and a prosecution, that the LPA was "entitled to take the view that given that this has not been remedied…we are now in the territory where the only legal step that is likely to make any difference and address the breach of planning control is the grant of an injunction". The failure to grant an injunction would mean that it "would effectively leave a serious and long-standing breach of planning control completely unaddressed and self-help would require public money to be spent" (paragraph 44(i)). The High Court referred to "a clear history of the Claimant trying different enforcement measures" and concluded that despite those measures, "it still continues to this day and clearly will simply continue as it has for several years now unless an injunction is granted" (paragraph 44(iii)). The High Court granted, therefore, the injunction sought which aimed to secure compliance with the terms of an extant Enforcement Notice. A similar approach was adopted by the High Court in *Chelmsford City Council & Braintree District Council v Mixture* [2024] EWHC 1006 (KB).

CHAPTER FIVE

CONSIDERATIONS IN SEEKING AN INJUNCTION

Necessary and Expedient

At paragraph 88 of *Ipswich*, Holgate J held that "an LPA cannot exercise the power to apply for an injunction under s.187B unless they consider it "necessary or expedient" to restrain a breach of planning control by injunction. Based on the clear language of the statute, it was common ground that the claimants in this case had to be satisfied not only that it was necessary or expedient to take enforcement action…but also that it was necessary or expedient to do so in this particular way, by seeking an injunction, rather than by other methods of enforcement".

As discussed above, this will be a key consideration for the LPA to address in its evidence. The analysis will be similar to, for example, that which one might expect to see in an Officer's Report recommending or authorising enforcement action.

Flagrancy

The caselaw is clear that "The "degree and flagrancy" of the breach of planning may be critical" (see paragraph 93 of *Ipswic*h citing *South Bucks*). The LPA will need to set out, therefore, in its evidence why it says the breach is a flagrant one. Flagrancy suggests a breach of planning control which is intentional, deliberate and wilful and one which was carried out with the knowledge that it was a breach. The High Court in *Buckinghamshire Council v Barrett* [2024] EWHC 140

(KB) said that, when considering flagrancy, "the proper context is to examine the course of conduct in breach of planning control as a whole" (paragraph 40) and that a "carefully timed and strategic breach" was a "flagrant" breach (paragraph 41).

For example, choosing to ignore the conditions subject to which a planning permission was granted might be considered flagrant as might carrying out the development over a bank holiday weekend in the hope it would be completed before the LPA became aware and could take any action. This will, therefore, be a fact sensitive analysis. Much will depend on, for example, the characteristics of the breach, the chronology of the breach and if, for example, the Defendant could have been expected to have professional advice or to otherwise have known that the development was a breach of planning control (a recently refused planning application for the same development would be one such example).

Further, a breach of planning control will also be a flagrant breach where it is "carried out in an area of environmental sensitivity or in an area subject to strong development control policies, such as the Green Belt" as per paragraph 117 of *Ipswich*.

Planning Harm

South Bucks indicates that it will be necessary for the Court to reach an overall view as the planning harm caused by the breach of planning control. It will be necessary, therefore, for the LPA to clearly set out what it says the planning harm of the unauthorised development is. This will require, therefore, the evidence to assess the relevant policies within the local development plan as well as national planning policy (including the National Planning Policy Framework, any relevant Written Ministerial Statements and, if relevant, the Planning Policy for Traveller Sites). The LPA will need to set out an assessment of those policies (which should be exhibited) and set out its view on why the development is one which is unacceptable and harmful in planning terms. This may be because it is development in the Green Belt and there are no Very Special Circumstances, or there may be ecological or environmental harm, or an impact on residential amenity of neighbours. Further, there may be landscape harm or heritage harm to be considered. Much will again depend on the particular facts of each case. It would be sensible for the LPA to make reference to the balancing exercise set out in section 38(6) of the Planning and Compulsory Purchase Act 2004 (although not strictly applicable), i.e. does the development accord with the statutory development plan read as a whole and do material considerations (including human rights, hardship and personal circumstances) indicate a decision other than in accordance with the development plan.

Human Rights

In *South Bucks*, at paragraph 31, it was held that "When an application is made to the Court under section 187B, the evidence will usually make clear whether, and to what extent, the local planning authority has taken account of the personal circumstances of the defendant and any hardship an injunction may cause. If it appears that these aspects have been neglected, and on examination they weigh against that grant of relief, the Court will be readier to refuse it. If it appears that the local planning authority has fully considered them and none the less resolved that it is necessary or expedient to seek relief, this will ordinarily weigh heavily in favour of granting relief, since the Court must accord respect to the balance which the local planning authority has struck between public and private interests".

Lord Scott also said in *South Bucks* that "The hardship likely to be caused to a defendant by the grant of an injunction to enforce the public law will always, in my opinion, be relevant to the court's decision whether or not to grant the injunction. In many, perhaps most, cases the hardship prayed in aid by the defendant will be of insufficient weight to counterbalance a continued and persistent disobedience to the law. There is a strong general public interest that planning controls should be observed and, if not observed, enforced. But each case must depend upon its own circumstances" (paragraph 102). The task for the Court, therefore, is to "weigh up the public interest in securing the enforcement of planning policy and planning decisions against the private interests of the individuals who are allegedly in breach of planning control" (paragraph 73 of *South Bucks*).

In *Vale of White Horse District Council v Winter* [2022] EWHC 2313 (QB), the High Court, at paragraph 18, held that the effect of the jurisprudence was that "since [a] injunction is a discretionary form of relief, I must not only be satisfied that the defendants have breached planning law but also that, in all of the circumstances, it is proportionate and just for the court to grant an injunction taking into account, amongst other things, the impact that such an injunction will have on the defendants some of whom are currently treating the land as their home, including their rights to private and family life under Article 8 of the European Convention on Human Rights".

The LPA will need, therefore, to clearly demonstrate in its evidence that it has considered the potential human rights implications, and the hardship which will be caused, and nonetheless resolved that an injunction is proportionate. It will need to clearly set out what rights it says are engaged, identify any interference with those rights and explain how it has concluded that the relief sought is proportionate. The range of rights which may be engaged is wide. For example, if there is residential occupation, plainly Article 8 ECHR will be engaged. There may be interference with property rights protected by Article One Protocol One. Further, if there is commercial activity, there may be interference with economic rights. If there are children living on a site, there may be interference with the right to an education. The LPA should also consider the best interests of the child as required by the Children Act 1989. The evidence will need to clearly demonstrate how all of this has been considered by the LPA.

That presupposes that the LPA has, at least, some knowledge of the personal circumstances of those involved in the breach of planning control. It should, for example, seek to obtain information through a welfare questionnaire where the breach is one involving unauthorised residential occupation. LPAs should also have regard to the duties, including the Public Sector Equality Duty, imposed by the Equality Act 2010.

CHAPTER SIX

INTERIM INJUNCTIONS

In many cases, the breach of planning control may arise suddenly. The LPA may wish to immediately secure or protect a site from further development or any development at all once it has become aware of the actual or apprehended breach of planning control. For example, a field in the Green Belt previously in an agricultural or equestrian use may quickly be the subject of a material change of use into a traveller site with hardstanding or hardcore laid to allow caravans or motorhomes to be placed on top. In those cases, the LPA will want to act quickly so as to ensure that the breach does not escalate by restraining any further development immediately and by restraining further occupants moving onto the land. Alternatively, it may have received information or a complaint that indicates that an unauthorised development is due to commence imminently. The LPA will want, in those cases, an injunction quickly to prevent the development taking place at all.

An interim injunction can be sought, therefore, to hold the ring pending the final determination of the application for a final section 187B injunction. The aim is to preserve the status quo and to restrain any further development, or any further intensification or increase in occupants, pending the final determination of the claim. It is, therefore, an extremely useful and powerful tool for a LPA who has discovered a breach of planning control. An interim injunction will only contain, therefore, restraining elements, i.e. "The Defendant must not carry out further development in breach of planning control", rather than mandatory elements, i.e. "The Defendant must remove the hardstanding placed on the land within three months of this order".

Holgate J, at paragraph 91 of *Ipswich*, confirmed that "the principles in *American Cyanamid Company v Ethicon* (No.1) [1975] AC 396 are applicable" when the Court is dealing with an application for an interim injunction. The *American Cyanamid* principles are:

(i) Is there is a triable issue?

(ii) Are damages an adequate remedy?

(iii) Where does the balance of convenience lie? This will include, as per paragraph 111 of *Ipswich*, consideration of whether immediate restraint by injunction, rather than the use of other enforcement action, would be "commensurate" with the harm.

The applicability of the *American Cyanamid* has important implications for the listing of the application for an interim injunction. The King's Bench Division Guide states that although Masters can, in principle, hear applications for interim injunction, where the application involves consideration of the *American Cyanamid* test, it will be listed before a High Court Judge (paragraph 11.3 of the Guide). The Guide elsewhere states, therefore, that "all applications for interim injunctions should be made to a High Court Judge" (paragraph 4.4).

The application for an interim injunction will need to be supported by evidence. Paragraph 3.2 of Practice Direction 25A tells us that the evidence can be set out in either a witness statement, a Statement of Case verified by a Statement of Truth or in the application itself provided that it is verified by a Statement of Truth. That evidence "must set out the facts on which the applicant relies for the claim being made against the respondent, including all material facts of which the court should be made aware" (paragraph 3.3).

Triable Issue

The Court will need to be satisfied that there is a serious question to be tried. This will be the case where the LPA can satisfactorily demonstrate that it is arguable that there has been an actual breach of planning control or that it is arguable that the proposed activity is an apprehended breach of planning control. In many cases, such as in *Ipswich*, this may be conceded by the Defendant at this stage (although the Defendant may indicate that despite that concession, it intends to contest the position that there is a breach at the final hearing).

Are damages an adequate remedy?

Section 187B injunctions are injunctions sought to enforce planning control and are an exercise of the LPA's statutory enforcement functions. It has been accepted, therefore, in the caselaw that damages would not be an adequate remedy for the LPA. In *Ipswich*, Holgate J, at paragraph 105, said that "There is no dispute that because each of the claimants is seeking to enforce planning control, damages could not be an adequate remedy. Indeed, I do not see how damages would even be an available remedy".

Equally, it has been accepted in the caselaw that, unlike in most other injunction cases, a cross undertaking in damages is not required from the LPA before an interim injunction can be granted. This is because the LPA is a public authority acting to uphold the public law. This principle was set out in *Kirklees Metropolitan Borough Council v Wickes Building Supplies Limited* [1993] AC 227 and was applied by the High Court in applications for interim injunctions in section 187B cases in, for example, *Ipswich* and *Great Yarmouth Borough Council v Al-Abdin* [2022] EWHC 3476 (KB). Equally, in *Wolverhampton City Council v London Gypsies and Travellers and others* [2023] UKSC 47 the Supreme Court said that "There is of course a principled reason why public bodies doing their public duty are relieved of this burden" (paragraph 182).

The balance of convenience

The Court will need to be satisfied that the balance of convenience lies in favour of granting injunctive relief. The High Court, at paragraph 93 of *Ipswich*, has confirmed that the principles set out in *South Bucks* will also be relevant when the Court is considering whether or not to grant an interim injunction. The evidence at the interim injunction stage should, therefore, address the issues and considerations raised by *South Bucks* (and in the later jurisprudence) as discussed above.

The approach adopted in *Ipswich* indicates that the balance of convenience is to be struck by reference to the planning harm caused (and the nature and extent of that harm). The LPA should, therefore, even at this early stage of the proceedings, set out in its evidence the analysis suggested above as to the planning harm of the development.

One of the important considerations will be, as per paragraph 111 of *Ipswich*, whether immediate restraint by an interim injunction, rather than the use of other enforcement action, would be "commensurate" with the alleged planning harm. In that paragraph of his judgment, Holgate J held that "The nature and extent of that harm also goes to the seriousness of the alleged breach and the urgency or otherwise of bringing it to an end". At paragraph 112 of *Ipswich*, he said that "The claimants accept that in each case the proposed use would not cause any environmental damage, or any harm to the amenity of neighbouring uses, or any harm to the character and appearance of the area. The buildings would not be altered. There would be no issues relating to traffic generation". Those factors weighed against, therefore, the grant of an interim injunction. The LPA will need to demonstrate, therefore, what the nature and extent of the harm is, why the breach is serious and why there is an urgent need to restrain it immediately by way of an interim injunction.

CHAPTER SEVEN

URGENT AND WITHOUT NOTICE APPLICATIONS FOR AN INTERIM INJUNCTION

Urgent Applications

In many cases the LPA will need to make an urgent application for an interim injunction. That has important procedural implications concerning the requirement to give notice of the application. An urgent application is not necessarily, however, an application without notice (discussed below) although in many cases the facts may be such as to warrant an urgent application to be made without any notice.

A High Court Judge will be available during term time, "both in normal hours and out of hours to deal with applications for interim remedies" (King's Bench Division Guide, paragraph 4.3). Each week a different Judge, who will sit in Court 37, will deal with urgent interim hearings which are likely to take an hour or less (paragraph 9.54). Applications which are likely to take longer than an hour will be assigned a hearing date and time (paragraph 9.56). Where there is a need to make an application out of hours, there will be a Duty Judge who will be available to deal with those applications. An application out of hours should only be made, however, where it is essential and those advising the LPA will need to consider their own professional obligations to ensure that they are satisfied that the case is one which is truly an urgent case which cannot wait until normal court hours (as the *Hamid* jurisdiction may be engaged). The High Court, in those cases, will require, therefore, "An explanation…as to why it was not made or could not be made during normal court hours" which "will require an explanation both of why the application was not made any earlier and why it cannot wait until the next sitting day so as to be dealt with by the duty Judge but within normal hours" (paragraph 11.19). See also paragraphs 11.18 to 11.24 of the King's Bench Division Guide for further information on the procedure to be followed when making an application out of hours. Those applications may be dealt with by way of a telephone hearing so long as "the applicant is acting by counsel or solicitors" (see paragraphs 4.3(3) and 4.5 of Practice Direction 25A).

The general rule, as per CPR r23.4, is that a copy of the application notice (which must state the order sought and the date, time and place of the hearing – see paragraph 2.1 of Practice Direction 25A) must be served on the Defendant (see below for a discussion of the circumstances in which it might be appropriate or necessary to make the application without notice). CPR 23.7(1) tells us that "A copy of the application notice must be served—(a) as soon as practicable after it is filed; and (b) at least 3 days before the court is to deal with the application unless a different time limit is stated in a rule, practice direction or court order". That suggests, therefore, that at least three days will be needed between the service of the application notice and the hearing. The application notice should be served alongside a copy of the supporting written evidence and a copy of any draft order prepared by the LPA (see CPR r23.7(3)).

It may not, however, always be possible in urgent cases to allow three days. In those cases, the Court can be asked, pursuant to CPR 23.7(4), to make an order that although "the period of notice is shorter than the period required by these Rules or a practice direction", "in the circumstances of the case, sufficient notice has been given" such that the Court "may hear the application". LPAs would be well advised, therefore, to do as much as they can to bring the application to the notice of the Defendants before it has been formally served and to do so as early as they can. The power under CPR 23.7(4) is a discretionary one and the LPA should bear in mind that the application may be refused, and the hearing listed at a time so as to allow the full amount of notice to be given. In general, it should only be in truly urgent cases, therefore, that the LPA should be asking the Court to abridge the notice period.

It is possible, in suitably urgent cases, to seek an interim injunction even prior to service of a Claim Form. Where an application has been made prior to issuing a Claim Form, there are specific procedural requirements which will apply as set out in paragraphs 4.3 and 4.4 of Practice Direction 25A. This includes, for example, the requirement, "unless the court orders otherwise", to provide an undertaking "to the court to issue a Claim Form immediately or the court will give directions for the commencement of the claim" (paragraph 4.41(1) of Practice Direction 25A).

Without Notice Applications

The LPA will need to consider whether the application should be made on notice to those involved in the actual or apprehended breach of planning control or whether the application should be made without notice, i.e. an ex parte application. This would mean that the first knowledge that those involved in the breach would have of the proceedings would come only after the application for an interim injunction had been heard by the High Court and, if granted, after an interim injunction was in place. This differs, therefore, from the situation in an urgent case as here no notice whatsoever, not even informal notice, would have been given. The general rule is as per CPR 23.4 is that notice should be given of the application. That may, however, not always be desirable and CPR 23.4 provides that notice is not required if "a rule, practice direction or court order permits otherwise". CPR 25.3(1) provides that an interim injunction may be granted "on an application made without notice if it appears to the court that there are good reasons for not giving notice".

An example of where the LPA might consider that notice is not desirable is if it considered that giving notice of the hearing might lead to further development or an intensification in the period between notice being given and the hearing taking place thereby defeating the purpose of the application for an interim injunction. That might be the case if, for example, the LPA was faced with an unauthorised traveller site development and considered that the effect of giving notice would be that others would quickly move onto the land before an injunction had been granted. It might also be the case if the LPA was aware that demolition works were due to take place at a certain time to enable a development and considered that if notice was given, the development would simply be carried out in advance of the hearing.

It is, however, a serious step for the High Court to grant an injunction without the Defendants having been allowed the opportunity to make submissions or to file evidence. CPR 25.3(3) requires, therefore, the LPA to make clear and explain in the evidence filed in support of the application "the reasons why notice has not been given". The High Court in *Ipswich* reaffirmed that "The general principle is that the court will not entertain an application of which no notice has been given, unless giving such notice would enable a defendant to take steps to defeat the purpose of the application…or there has been no time at all to give notice before an injunction is required to prevent the threatened act" and said that the grant of an injunction without notice is "an exceptional remedy" (paragraph 64).

Paragraph 4.3(3) of Practice Direction 25A says, therefore, that "except in cases where secrecy is essential, the applicant should take steps to notify the respondent informally of the application". This was referred to by the High Court in *Ipswich* which said that "Modern methods of communication make it unlikely that there will ever be a practical justification for not giving informal notice of the application and documentation relied upon" (paragraph 63).

The LPA will need, therefore, to clearly explain why the facts are such as to justify not giving notice and, in particular, why secrecy is necessary. The Court will subject the LPA's reasoning to some scrutiny, and it may also be scrutinised at a later stage in the proceedings by a Defendant. This exercise, therefore, cannot simply be a perfunctory one as justified and evidenced reasons must exist to justify not giving any notice at all. Those acting for the LPA should also be aware that there are professional obligations upon them to ensure that there is a proper justification for the application being made without notice.

The duty of candour and to provide full and frank disclosure will apply with particular force where an application is made without notice. Any failure to comply with those duties, e.g. a failure to provide the Court with any information the LPA has as to the personal circumstances of occupants, could lead to the interim injunction being discharged at a later stage with costs consequences. The High Court in *Ipswich* was clear that "Applicants for *ex parte* injunctions need also to be mindful of the practical implications of not giving notice to a respondent. In such circumstances, a claimant (including those representing him) is under a duty owed to the court to make a full and frank disclosure of all matters relevant to the application, including all matters of fact or law which are or may be adverse to the claimant (Civil Procedure at para 25.3.5). If that duty is not fulfilled, the court may discharge the injunction obtained *ex parte* (Civil Procedure at para. 25.3.6). There may also be other consequences" (paragraph 65).

This is reaffirmed by the King's Bench Division Guide which says that "it is the duty of the applicant to fully disclose all matters relevant to the application, including those matters adverse to the applicant. The application must specifically direct the court to those passages in the evidence which disclose matters adverse to the application. Failure to do so may result in the order being set aside" (paragraph 11.9).

The LPA will be required to provide an undertaking to "serve on the respondent the application notice, evidence in support and any order made as soon as practicable" (paragraph 5.1(2) of Practice Direction 25A). The application and supporting evidence must be served even if the application for a without notice interim injunction was unsuccessful – see CPR 23.9(2).

The High Court, if minded to grant an interim injunction without notice, will generally only grant the interim injunction for a limited time period. It will generally list a return date hearing a few days or a week after the initial hearing so that the Defendant can be given notice of the hearing and participate in the proceedings (see paragraph 5.1(3) of Practice Direction 25A). The Court will then consider whether or not to continue the interim injunction which had been granted at the initial hearing.

Where an application has been made without notice, and an interim injunction is granted, the Defendant may make a subsequent application to have that order set aside or varied. Any application "must, unless the court directs otherwise, be made within 7 days after the date on which the order was served on the person making the application" – see CPR 23.10.

CHAPTER EIGHT

PRACTICAL MATTERS

Form of the proceedings

Although section 187B(4) refers to the County Court, the need for the High Court to consider any application for an interim injunction requiring the application of the *American Cyanamid* principles means that, in practice, a large number of section 187B applications will be determined in the High Court. The general practice is for LPAs to rely on the procedure set out in Part 8 of the CPR which is an alternative procedure for claims and is a more simplified route than Part 7 for the determination of the claim. This is because paragraph 4.4 of Practice Direction 49E assigns applications pursuant to section 187B of the 1990 Act to Part 8 (and, in particular, the King's Bench Division rather than the Planning Court list within the Administrative Court). Any defendant may, however, object, when filing its Acknowledgement of Service, to the use of the Part 8 procedure (pursuant to CPR 8.8(1)). The Part 8 procedure means that, inter alia, the default judgment procedure is not available to the LPA.

Multiple LPA Areas

From time to time, there may be a site which straddles the boundary of two local planning authorities. The question in that situation is which of the LPAs should take action or if one LPA can take action on behalf of another? The High Court confirmed in *R (Parkes) v Dorset Council* [2024] EWHC 1253 (Admin) that a LPA cannot take enforcement action against a breach of planning control outside its boundaries, even where that unauthorised development has an impact inside its area (paragraphs 196-202). The correct approach, therefore, would be either for both LPAs to be Claimants (as was the case in *Chelmsford City Council & Braintree District Council v Mixture* [2024] EWHC 1006 (KB)) or, alternatively, for one LPA to delegate its authority to seek an injunction to the other LPA pursuant to section 101(1) of the Local Government Act 1972.

The problem with the latter approach, however, although it seems attractive at first blush, is that the Court will need evidence of the planning harm arising through conflict with relevant development plan policies and the development plan will be different in each local authority area. The most pragmatic approach would, therefore, appear to be for both to be Claimants and for witness statements to be provided on behalf of each setting out the particular planning considerations applicable in each area. There may, however, be situations in which delegation is appropriate, e.g. if it is only a very small part of the site which falls outside the boundary of one LPA and the planning harm is obvious, e.g. inappropriate development in the Green Belt.

Defendants

It will be necessary to ensure that the correct parties are joined to the proceedings (not least because the LPA may face an application for costs from any parties incorrectly joined to the proceedings who have incurred unnecessary costs). In some cases, the correct Defendant may simply be the landowner or, for example, the parties on whom an Enforcement Notice was served. A useful starting point will be, therefore, to consult the Land Registry although LPAs should be aware that there is often a delay in the title documents being updated such that it is not always accurate. The LPA should also consider any planning applications submitted in connection with the land. In many cases, however, the situation will be more complicated. If the breach of planning control is the unauthorised use of the land for vehicle sales and car parking, as was the case in *Hillingdon LBC v Harlington Investors Ltd* [2024] 11 WLUK 262, or some other commercial use, there may be many parties involved in the unauthorised use of the land who should all be joined to the proceedings. Equally, where the unauthorised use is a residential use, the LPA, in addition to any landowner or tenant who has allowed or facilitated the use, should seek to join each of the residents of the site.

The LPA should set out in its evidence what efforts it has made to identify the parties involved in the breach of planning control and should explain precisely why each of the Defendants has been joined to the proceedings.

If it subsequently comes to light that a party has been joined incorrectly, the LPA should exercise its right, pursuant to CPR 38.2(1), to discontinue the claim against that defendant. It should do so by, pursuant to CPR 38.2, filing a Notice of Discontinuance and serving that on "every other party to the proceedings". This will limit the exposure of the LPA to an adverse costs order.

Equally, if the identity of another party involved in the breach of planning control, or somehow responsible for the breach, comes to light, the LPA can, pursuant to CPR 19.4(1), ask the Court for permission to "add or substitute a party". An application might also be made where the ownership of the land has changed during the lifetime of the proceedings or a new tenant or party has moved onto the land. Any application will, however, need to be supported by evidence and should be made under Part 23 – see CPR 19.4(2)(b). The Court will need to consider if it desirable to add or substitute the new party to resolve the matters in dispute in the proceedings.

Persons Unknown

Section 187B(3) of the 1990 Act provides that "Rules of court may provide for such an injunction to be issued against a person whose identity is unknown". Paragraph 21.2 of Practice Direction 49E provides that where an application is made under section 187B of the 1990 Act, "An injunction may be granted under those sections against a person whose identity is unknown to the applicant".

At the outset, LPAs should be aware that there is, in effect, two categories of Persons Unknown which may be engaged in section 187B cases, which raise different considerations. The first category is where the LPA is simply unaware of who the protagonists, or all of the protagonists, involved in a breach of planning control are. An unauthorised commercial site may be occupied, for example, by multiple businesses and traders and it may not have been possible to identify all of the individuals and/or corporate entities involved in the unauthorised use so as to join them to the proceedings. Or the LPA may be unaware as to the identity of the person who directed the operational development to be carried out or the identify of those involved in carrying out the works. The second category is where the LPA wants an injunction to restrain those who might become involved in the breach of planning control in the future, i.e. newcomers. This will most commonly arise in situations where the LPA is faced with an unauthorised gypsy or traveller site and wishes to restrain any newcomers who may wish to move onto the site in the future. Those newcomers will be unknown and unidentified at the date the Order is made and will not yet have performed or threatened to perform the acts restrained by the injunction. It is the second category which gives rise to the most concern, therefore, for the Court as, inter alia, those individuals will not have been aware of the proceedings at all and will not have had the opportunity to make any submissions to the Court prior to the injunction being granted.

The Court of Appeal, in *London Borough of Barking & Dagenham v Persons Unknown & Ors* [2022] EWCA Civ 13 ("***Barking & Dagenham***"), had the opportunity to review the caselaw on the availability of injunctions against persons unknown. The Court of Appeal, at paragraph 117, said that where the application is for an injunction pursuant to section 187B of the 1990 Act, "the applicant must describe any persons unknown in the claim form by reference to photographs, things belonging to them or any other evidence, and that description must be sufficiently clear to enable persons unknown to be served with the proceedings, whilst acknowledging that the court retains the power in appropriate cases to dispense with service or to permit service by an alternative method or at an alternative place. These safeguards and those referred to with approval earlier in this judgment are as much applicable to an injunction sought in an unauthorised encampment cases under section 187B as they are to one sought in such a case to restrain apprehended trespass or nuisance". The Court of Appeal was reflecting, therefore, paragraph 21.4 of Practice Direction 49E which states that where an application is made under section 187B of the 1990 Act, and an injunction is sought against Persons Unknown, "In the claim form, the applicant must describe the defendant by reference to – (1) a photograph; (2) a thing belonging to or in the possession of the defendant; or (3) any other evidence". Paragraph 21.5 states categorically that "The description of the defendant under paragraph 20.4 must be sufficiently clear to enable the defendant to be served with the proceedings".

The LPA is required, by virtue of paragraph 21.6 of Practice Direction 49E, to state in a Witness Statement that "that the applicant was unable to ascertain the defendant's identity within the time reasonably available to him" and to set out "the steps taken by him to ascertain the defendant's identity", "the means by which the defendant has been described in the claim form" and that "that the description is the best the applicant is able to provide".

The Supreme Court in *Wolverhampton City Council v London Gypsies and Travellers and others* [2023] UKSC 47 ("***Wolverhampton***") was concerned with an appeal against, inter alia, *Barking & Dagenham.* The focus of the Supreme Court was, therefore, on applications for final section 187B injunctions which sought to restrain activities by Persons Unknown in the context of gypsy and traveller cases. The Supreme Court said that "The emphasis in this discussion has been on newcomer injunctions in Gypsy and Traveller cases and nothing we have said should be taken as prescriptive in relation to newcomer injunctions in other cases" (paragraph 235). The Supreme Court confirmed, however, that ""In so far as the local authorities are seeking to prevent breaches of public law, including planning law...they are empowered to seek injunctions by statutory provisions...They can accordingly invoke the equitable jurisdiction of the court, which extends, as we have explained, to the granting of newcomer injunctions" (paragraph 170). *Wolverhampton* has resolved, therefore, the long running debate as to whether or not the Courts have the jurisdiction to grant newcomer injunctions by confirming that such a power does exist.

Wolverhampton will be extremely important (and often determinative) in cases involving gypsies and travellers (and, it is suggested, travelling showpeople) where the LPA seeks an injunction to restrain newcomers. *Wolverhampton* was first applied (shortly after it was handed down) in the context of an application for a section 187B injunction concerning travellers by the High Court in *Buckinghamshire Council v Barrett* [2024] EWHC 140 (KB) where the High Court described it as an "important authority" (paragraph 10).

In *Wolverhampton*, the Supreme Court made the following important points which must be borne in mind by the LPA (which relate both to the substantive power to grant such an injunction and also to the procedural safeguards which ought to be secured so as to protect the rights and interests of those likely to be affected):

(i) There is a practical need for newcomer injunctions (paragraph 131) which are "in substance always a type of without notice injunction, whether in form interim or final" (paragraph 142) although "informal notice of the application for such an injunction may nevertheless be given by advertisement" (paragraph 143(ii)).

(ii) There is "no immoveable obstacle in the way of granting injunctions against newcomer Travellers, on an essentially without notice basis, regardless of whether in form interim or final, either in terms of jurisdiction or principle. But this by no means leads straight to the conclusion that they ought to be granted, either generally or on the facts of any particular case" (paragraph 167).

(iii) Such an injunction is "only likely to be justified as a novel exercise of an equitable discretionary power" if: "There is a compelling need, sufficiently demonstrated by the evidence, for the…enforcement of planning control…in the locality which is not adequately met by any other measures available to the applicant local authorities (including the making of byelaws)"; "There is procedural protection for the rights (including Convention rights) of the affected newcomers, sufficient to overcome the strong prima facie objection of subjecting them to a without notice injunction otherwise than as an emergency measure to hold the ring. This will need to include an obligation to take all reasonable steps to draw the application and any order made to the attention of all those likely to be affected by it…and the most generous provision for liberty (ie permission) to apply to have the injunction varied or set aside, and on terms that the grant of the injunction in the meantime does not foreclose any objection of law, practice, justice or convenience which the newcomer so applying might wish to raise"; the LPA complies with "the most stringent form of disclosure duty on making an application, so as both to research for and then present to the court everything that might have been said by the targeted newcomers against the grant of injunctive relief"; and "The injunctions are constrained by both territorial and temporal limitations so as to ensure, as far as practicable, that they neither outflank nor outlast the compelling circumstances relied upon" (paragraph 167).

(iv) The question of "whether byelaws or other such measures or powers represent a workable alternative…is one which should be addressed on a case by case basis" (paragraph 172).

The LPA will need to set out in "detailed evidence", therefore, "that there is a compelling justification for the order sought" against newcomers in a gypsy and traveller case (*Wolverhampton* at paragraph 188). This raises the test, therefore, for the grant of a section 187B injunction as the LPA is not otherwise required to demonstrate a compelling justification for the remedy. The LPA will also need to set out evidence of whether it "has complied with its obligations (such as they are) properly to consider and provide lawful stopping places for Gypsies and Travellers within the geographical areas for which it is responsible", whether it "has exhausted all reasonable alternatives to the grant of an injunction, including whether it has engaged in a dialogue with the Gypsy and Traveller communities to try to find a way to accommodate their nomadic way of life by giving them time and assistance to find alternative or transit sites, or more permanent accommodation" and "whether the authority has taken appropriate steps to control or even prohibit unauthorised encampments and related activities by using the other measures and powers at its disposal" (paragraph 189 of *Wolverhampton*). The Supreme Court said that "A failure by the local authority in one or more of these respects may make it more difficult to satisfy a court that the relief it seeks is just and convenient" (paragraph 189).

The Supreme Court went on to say that demonstrating a compelling justification means that "There must be a strong probability that a tort or breach of planning control or other aspect of public law is to be committed and that this will cause real harm. Further, the threat must be real and imminent" (paragraph 218). The LPA will need, therefore, to carefully set out why this is the case in its evidence. This is extremely important if the application is to be successful (and to avoid the conclusion that the application was not well founded). In *Buckinghamshire Council v Barrett* [2024] EWHC 140 (KB), the High Court held that "When the claimant speaks in mere "possibilities" and not higher degrees of likelihood, the court cannot grant an injunction against Persons Unknown. The risk is too indistinct, uncertain and conjectural" (paragraph 80).

As to the drafting of the order, the Supreme Court in *Wolverhampton* said that "It is always important that an injunction spells out clearly and in everyday terms the full extent of the acts it prohibits, and this is particularly so where it is sought against persons unknown, including newcomers. The terms of the injunction – and therefore the prohibited acts – must correspond as closely as possible to the actual or threatened unlawful conduct. Further, the order should extend no further than the minimum necessary to achieve the purpose for which it was granted; and the terms of the order must be sufficiently clear and precise to enable persons affected by it to know what they must not do" (paragraph 222 of *Wolverhampton*). As to the "need for strict temporal and territorial limits", the Supreme Court said that "We have considerable doubt as to whether it could ever be justifiable to grant a Gypsy or Traveller injunction which is directed to persons unknown, including newcomers, and extends over the whole of a borough or for significantly more than a year" (paragraph 225). The Supreme Court also said that "injunctions of this kind must be reviewed periodically…and in our view ought to come to an end (subject to any order of the judge), by effluxion of time in all cases after no more than a year unless an application is made for their renewal. This will give all parties an opportunity to make full and complete disclosure to the court, supported by appropriate evidence, as to how effective the order has been; whether any reasons or grounds for its discharge have emerged; whether there is any proper justification for its continuance; and whether and on what basis a further order ought to be made" (paragraph 225 of *Wolverhampton*).

As to advertisement of the application, the Supreme Court said that "in the interests of procedural fairness, we consider that any local authority intending to make an application of this kind must take reasonable steps to draw the application to the attention of persons likely to be affected by the injunction sought or with some other genuine and proper interest in the application…This should be done in sufficient time before the application is heard to allow those persons (or those representing them or their interests) to make focused submissions as to whether it is appropriate for an injunction to be granted and, if it is, as to the terms and conditions of any such relief" (paragraph 226 of *Wolverhampton*). The steps taken by the LPA will have to be explained in its evidence (see paragraphs 228 and 231).

The order should "include generous liberty to any person affected by its terms to apply to vary or discharge the whole or any part of the order" irrespective of whether it is an interim or final injunction (paragraph 232 of *Wolverhampton*).

As to other cases where injunctions are sought against Persons Unknown who are not gypsies or travellers, the Supreme Court was clear that "in so far as the applicant seeks an injunction against newcomers, the judge must be satisfied there is a compelling need for the order. Often the circumstances of these cases vary significantly one from another in terms of the range and number of people who may be affected by the making or refusal of the injunction sought; the legal right to be protected; the illegality to be prevented; and the rights of the respondents to the application. The duration and geographical scope of the injunction necessary to protect the applicant's rights in any particular case are ultimately matters for the judge having regard to the general principles we have explained" (paragraph 236).

Where an interim injunction is granted against Persons Unknown, it is likely that the Court will require wording to be included in the order which directs the LPA, should it become aware of the identity of any of the persons encapsulated within Persons Unknown, to make an application to join that person as a named Defendant to the proceedings.

Service

CPR Part 6 governs the important issue of service. The Court will want to ensure that the necessary documents have been served on the Defendant so as to allow the Defendant to have notice of the proceedings and to enable the Defendant to be heard before the final determination of the application. Certificates of Service will therefore assist the Court. It will be a question of fact as to whether or not the contents of the document served have come to the attention of the Defendant (see *Wolverhampton* at paragraph 115).

Where Persons Unknown are involved, however, and as the Supreme Court recognised in *Wolverhampton*, "Conventional methods of service may be impractical where defendants cannot be identified" (paragraph 56). Even where all the Defendants have been identified, the LPA may consider it desirable or more expedient to not have to serve each of those Defendants individually and may want to ask the Court to allow it to serve, for example, at the land in question.

The Court has the power, pursuant to CPR 6.15, to "make an order permitting service [of the Claim Form] by an alternative method or at an alternative place". The Court will have to be satisfied, however, "that there is a good reason to authorise service by a method or at a place not otherwise permitted by this Part" – see CPR 6.15(1). An application supported by evidence will be required – see CPR 6.16(3). There are specific procedural requirements for any order made by the Court – see CPR 6.15(4). The nature of such an order is likely to be that the Claim Form, or other documents, or any Order made is to be served by the LPA fixing copies in conspicuous locations at the land. It is only in exceptional circumstances that the Court will dispense with the requirement to dispense with service of the Claim Form entirely – see CPR 6.16.

CPR 6.27 extends the power to order service by an alternative method or at any alternative place "to any document in the proceedings". An order could be made, therefore, in respect of any injunction granted.

It is important that any order granted makes clear that, for the purposes of CPR Part 81 (Contempt Proceedings), pursuant to CPR 81.4(2)(c), the need for personal service was dispensed with by the Court.

Uncooperative Defendants

LPAs may often face uncooperative Defendants who choose to ignore or otherwise not participate in the proceedings. They may choose not to, for example, file any evidence. Often the Defendant may choose not to attend, or be represented at, the final hearing of the application for a final injunction. In those circumstances, the Court can, pursuant to CPR 23.11(1), proceed in their absence.

In *Chelmsford City Council & Braintree District Council v Mixture* [2024] EWHC 1006 (KB), an adjournment had been sought by way of an email sent to the LPA's solicitors during the weekend immediately prior to the hearing of the application for a final injunction. This was refused by the High Court who noted, inter alia, that "there was no formal adjournment application....supported by evidence from the Defendant" who "was aware of these proceedings and the hearing date" (paragraph 10). The High Court concluded that "Adjournments not only waste time and money but they also cause prejudice to other litigants whose cases have to wait in line" and held that "In all the circumstances, it would not be consistent with the overriding objective for this trial to be adjourned. Fairness does not require an adjournment" (paragraph 11).

Extant planning applications or appeals

In some cases, the Defendant may have either submitted a planning application (either a retrospective application or an application submitted prior to the implementation of the unauthorised development) to the LPA or may be in the progress of progressing an appeal to the Secretary of State against the refusal of planning permission. The Defendant may also be progressing a ground (a) appeal against an Enforcement Notice issued by the LPA which, if successful, would result in a grant of planning permission for the breach of planning control the subject of the notice. The question arises, therefore, as to what the Court should do in those circumstances. Should it continue to determine the application and potentially grant a final injunction where there is, at least, the potential for planning permission to be granted (assuming that the breach of planning control the subject of the section 187B application corresponds, at least in part, with the development for which planning permission may be granted). This may be fertile ground for the Defendant to resist the imposition of an injunction, i.e. by arguing that the planning merits are not yet settled and that it may be the case that planning permission will be granted (thereby demonstrating that the unauthorised development is acceptable in planning terms and/or that the LPA's case on planning harm was overstated).

The decision in *Chelmsford City Council v Lee* [2019] EWHC 756 (QB) will assist. In that case, there weas an extant appeal against the refusal of planning permission which was likely to be determined within 12 months (paragraph 35). The High Court held that the judgment in *South Bucks* "does not require me to evaluate the prospects of success of an appeal, but it would only be sensible for the court not to shut its mind to the possibility of an appeal being successful, but it is not, in my judgment, for me to evaluate the real chances of success" (paragraph 46). The High Court was minded there to accept undertakings rather than to grant an injunction for a number of reasons, including the fact that the breach was not flagrant and leaving "now, in the light of the pending appeal, would cause very significant disruption" (see paragraphs 64-72). The undertakings there were to "abide by the outcome of the planning appeal to the inspector, to comply with the conditions if he granted permission and to leave the land and take up the hardstanding if he did not, and not to seek to challenge his decision further" (paragraph 69).

The decision, therefore, will depend on the particular circumstances of the case. It is not always the case that the mere existence of an extant application planning appeal will be enough to secure an adjournment or a delayed execution of the final injunction. Much will depend on, for example, whether undertakings have been provided by the Defendants. It might be possible, however, for wording to be agreed in a Consent Order between the LPA and the Defendants which, for example, only requires the mandatory steps, i.e. the removal or cessation of the unauthorised development and the remediation of the land, within a certain period of time from the refusal of the application or appeal (and for the mandatory steps to fall away if planning permission is required). Similar wording might also be imposed by the Court following a contested hearing. In other cases, the breach might be so flagrant or the prospects of planning permission being granted so low that the Court will grant a final injunction irrespective of the fact there is an extant application or appeal (although noting that it is not for the Court to become involved in matters of planning judgment, the Court should still accord respect to the views of the LPA).

Costs

The general rule, as per CPR 44.2(2)(a), is that "that the unsuccessful party will be ordered to pay the costs of the successful party". If the LPA is successful in its application, it can ask the Court for an order that the Defendant pays its costs. Equally, if the Defendant successfully resists the application, it can ask the Court to make an order that the LPA pays its costs. The Court always retains, however, a discretion and can depart from that general rule, and make whatever order it considers appropriate, in suitable cases.

CHAPTER NINE

CONSIDERATIONS IN RESPONDING TO AN APPLICATION FOR AN INJUNCTION

CPR 8.3(1) provides that any Defendant must "file an acknowledgment of service in the relevant practice form not more than 14 days after service of the claim form" and "serve the acknowledgment of service on the claimant and any other party". CPR 8.3(2) requires the Defendant to state, in the Acknowledgement of Service, whether it contests the claim for a section 187B injunction. A failure to file an Acknowledgment of Service will have serious consequences for the Defendant as if a Defendant fails to do so, and the time period for doing so has expired, CPR 8.4(2) provides that "The defendant may attend the hearing of the claim but may not take part in the hearing unless the court gives permission". CPR 8.4(3) further provides that "A defendant who wishes to rely on written evidence must file it when they file their acknowledgment of service" (and the LPA will have 14 days from the date on which the evidence was served to reply – CPR 8.5(5)). As the claim is most likely to be a Part 8 claim (unless the Defendant objects and the Court agrees), there will be no requirement, therefore, for a Defence.

Extensions of time can be sought, however, for the filing and serving of evidence – see CPR 8.5(8). It may also be possible to agree an extension with the other parties – see CPR 8.5(9) and 8.5(10). It is also possible that the Court, at the hearing of the application for an interim injunction, makes directions setting a different timetable for the filing and serving of evidence and the listing of the final hearing (and LPAs generally suggest draft directions in the draft order).

Again, the failure to file any evidence will have serious consequences for any Defendant as CPR 8.6(1) provides that no written evidence may be relied upon at the hearing unless it has been served in accordance with CPR 8.5, or the Court gives permission. The power under CPR 8.5(1)(b) is a discretionary power and the Court may not always grant permission. It is optimal, therefore, for the Defendant to seek to comply with the CPR and/or any directions made by the Court. It is essential for any Defendant to ensure that it puts before the Court evidence of what hardship would be caused by the grant of an injunction. This will assist the Court in considering whether or not to grant an injunction.

CHAPTER TEN

WHAT HAPPENS IF AN INJUNCTION IS NOT OBEYED?

The failure to abide by the terms of an injunction is a contempt of court. This reflects the fact that an injunction is an order of the Court, and it is, therefore, extremely serious if it not strictly abided by. CPR Part 81 sets out the procedure to be followed in applications and proceedings in relation to contempt of court. LPAs, and those involved in drafting the order, should be aware of the need to include a Penal Notice on the front of the order, i.e. a "prominent notice added to the front of an order by or at the request of a party warning that if the person against whom the order is made (and, in the case of a corporate body, a director or officer of that body) disobeys the court's order, the person (or director or officer) may be held in contempt of court and punished by a fine, imprisonment, confiscation of assets or other punishment under the law" (see CPR 81.2). The fact that the breach of a section 187B injunction (or an interim injunction) can result in imprisonment highlights the powerful nature of such an injunction and is a fact likely to focus the minds of those involved in even the most flagrant of breaches of planning control.

A person who is not a party to the proceedings, and not the subject of the order, may also face contempt proceedings where, as Lord Oliver held in in *Attorney General v Times Newspapers Ltd* [1992] 1 AC 191, the non-party "frustrates, thwarts, or subverts the purpose of the court's order and thereby interferes with the due administration of justice in the particular action". Non-parties can, therefore, be referred to "in an injunction in order to indicate the breadth of its binding effect" because of the fact that "non-parties can be found in contempt of court for acting contrary to an injunction" (paragraph 41 of *Wolverhampton*). The Supreme Court was clear, therefore, in *Wolverhampton* that "even where an injunction enjoins a named individual, the public at large are bound not knowingly to subvert it" (paragraph 42).

CHAPTER ELEVEN

CONCLUSION

This book has demonstrated that the statutory power afforded to the LPA by section 187B of the 1990 Act is a powerful and versatile remedy. The caselaw discussed throughout demonstrates, however, that it is one which should only be exercised where properly justified and where an injunction is actually required. The jurisprudence illustrates that the LPA will need to properly present a case of real planning harm to the Court and to persuade it that it is necessary and expedient for an injunction to be granted. The Court will not simply defer to the views of the LPA and grant an injunction simply because the LPA says it should. This is because the jurisdiction is an original one, and not a supervisory one, and the Court retains the ultimate discretion as to whether an order should be granted at all, and if so, what the terms of that order should be.

This book has set out the considerations which ought to be considered by the LPA in deciding whether or not to seek an injunction and also in the evidence it puts before the Court. Where an application is properly founded and justified, a section 187B injunction will be a powerful tool in restraining and, where necessary, remediating harmful breaches of planning control. The facts of the cases discussed in this book illustrate the broad range of situations in which a section 187B injunction may prove of assistance. Nevertheless, it has also illustrated that in some situations, an injunction may be refused if, for example, the hardship relied on by a Defendant is such as to outweigh the public interest in enforcing planning control (although it has been demonstrated that that will be a rare situation – see *South Bucks* at paragraph 102). That may be fertile ground for a Defendant to seek to resist the imposition of an injunction (as will any suggestion that other enforcement powers would be more appropriate than an injunction).

This book has also demonstrated that section 187B injunctions give rise to a number of practical procedural considerations, e.g. as to service, which must be carefully navigated by LPAs and Defendants alike. This is particularly the case where an application is urgent, or made without notice, or relates to Persons Unknown. Those advising LPAs and Defendants alike will need to have an intimate knowledge of the CPR.

This book is commended, therefore, to all those who find themselves in the situation of considering whether or not to seek an injunction as well as those who find themselves resisting the grant of an injunction. It is hoped that it will be a useful and practical guide to this exciting and evolving area of planning law.

MORE BOOKS BY LAW BRIEF PUBLISHING

A selection of our other titles available now:-

'A Practical Guide to Probation Breaches and Other Applications' by Mark Thomas
'A Practical Guide to Remarriage and Divorce' by Cordelia Williams & Claire Howard
'A Practical Guide to Privacy, Transparency, Reporting Restrictions and Closed Proceedings in the Court of Protection' by Laura Mannering
'Beaumont on Barristers – A Guide to Defending Disciplinary Proceedings (Second Edition)' by Marc Beaumont
'A Practical Guide to Payments for Environmental Services' by Ben Sharples
'A Practical Guide to the Law of Pregnancy and Maternity at Work' by Rebecca Thomas
'A Practical Guide to Redundancy – Second Edition' by Philip Hyland & Collette Moore
'A Practical Guide to International Issues for Scottish Family Lawyers' by Susie Mountain, Donna McKay, Ken MacDonald
'A Practical Guide to the Law on Deprivation of Liberty' by Ben Troke
'A Practical Guide to Rights over Airspace and Subsoil – Second Edition' by Daniel Gatty
'A Practical Guide to the Law in Relation to Inquests' by Ramya Nagesh
'A Practical Guide to the Construction and Rectification of Wills and Trust Instruments (Second Edition)' by Edward Hewitt
'A Practical Guide to Data Protection in Social Housing' by Clare Paterson
'A Practical Guide to Spousal Maintenance – Second Edition' by Liz Cowell
'A Practical Guide to International Parental Child Abduction Law (England and Wales)' by Dr Onyója Momoh
'A Practical Guide to Deprivation of British Citizenship' by Sean Ell
'A Practical Guide to Commercial Property Service Charges' by Rachel Garton
'A Practical Guide to Clinical Negligence – Third Edition' by Geoffrey Simpson-Scott (Geoff)
'A Practical Guide to the Rights of Grandparents in Children Proceedings – Second Edition' by Stuart Barlow

'The Electronic Communications Code: A Practical Guide – Second Edition' by Kerry Bretherton KC, James Castle, Mark Loveday
'A Practical Guide to the Independent School Standards – September 2023 Edition' by Sarah McKimm
'A Practical Guide to Estate Administration and Crypto Assets' by Richard Marshall
'A Practical Guide to Parental Alienation in Private and Public Law Children Cases' by Sam King QC & Frankie Shama
'Contested Heritage – Removing Art from Land and Historic Buildings' by Richard Harwood QC, Catherine Dobson, David Sawtell
'The Limits of Separate Legal Personality: When Those Running a Company Can Be Held Personally Liable for Losses Caused to Third Parties Outside of the Company' by Dr Mike Wilkinson
'A Practical Guide to Transgender Law' by Robin Moira White & Nicola Newbegin
'A Practical Guide to 'Stranded Spouses' in Family Law' by Mani Singh Basi
'A Practical Guide to Residential Freehold Conveyancing' by Lorraine Richardson
'A Practical Guide to Pensions on Divorce for Lawyers' by Bryan Scant
'A Practical Guide to Challenging Sham Marriage Allegations in Immigration Law' by Priya Solanki
'A Practical Guide to Digital Communications Evidence in Criminal Law' by Sam Willis
'A Practical Guide to Legal Rights in Scotland' by Sarah-Jane Macdonald
'A Practical Guide to New Build Conveyancing' by Paul Sams & Rebecca East
'A Practical Guide to Inherited Wealth on Divorce' by Hayley Trim
'A Practical Guide to Practice Direction 12J and Domestic Abuse in Private Law Children Proceedings' by Rebecca Cross & Malvika Jaganmohan
'A Practical Guide to Confiscation and Restraint' by Narita Bahra QC, John Carl Townsend, David Winch
'A Practical Guide to the Law of Forests in Scotland' by Philip Buchan
'A Practical Guide to Health and Medical Cases in Immigration Law' by Rebecca Chapman & Miranda Butler
'A Practical Guide to Bad Character Evidence for Criminal Practitioners by Aparna Rao
'A Practical Guide to Extradition Law post-Brexit' by Myles Grandison et al
'A Practical Guide to Hoarding and Mental Health for Housing Lawyers' by Rachel Coyle

'Stephens on Contractual Indemnities' by Richard Stephens
'A Practical Guide to the EU Succession Regulation' by Richard Frimston
'A Practical Guide to Solicitor and Client Costs – Second Edition' by Robin Dunne
'Constructive Dismissal – Practice Pointers and Principles' by Benjimin Burgher
'A Practical Guide to Religion and Belief Discrimination Claims in the Workplace' by Kashif Ali
'A Practical Guide to the Law of Medical Treatment Decisions' by Ben Troke
'Fundamental Dishonesty and QOCS in Personal Injury Proceedings: Law and Practice' by Jake Rowley
'A Practical Guide to the Law in Relation to School Exclusions' by Charlotte Hadfield & Alice de Coverley
'A Practical Guide to Divorce for the Silver Separators' by Karin Walker
'The Right to be Forgotten – The Law and Practical Issues' by Melissa Stock
'A Practical Guide to Planning Law and Rights of Way in National Parks, the Broads and AONBs' by James Maurici QC, James Neill et al
'A Practical Guide to Election Law' by Tom Tabori
'A Practical Guide to the Law in Relation to Surrogacy' by Andrew Powell
'A Practical Guide to Claims Arising from Fatal Accidents – Second Edition' by James Patience
'A Practical Guide to Asbestos Claims' by Jonathan Owen & Gareth McAloon
'A Practical Guide to Stamp Duty Land Tax in England and Northern Ireland' by Suzanne O'Hara
'A Practical Guide to the Law of Farming Partnerships' by Philip Whitcomb
'A Practical Guide to the Law of Unlawful Eviction and Harassment – Second Edition' by Stephanie Lovegrove
'A Practical Guide to Costs in Personal Injury Claims – Second Edition' by Matthew Hoe
'A Practical Guide to the General Data Protection Regulation (GDPR) – Second Edition' by Keith Markham
'A Practical Guide to Working with Litigants in Person and McKenzie Friends in Family Cases' by Stuart Barlow
'Protecting Unregistered Brands: A Practical Guide to the Law of Passing Off' by Lorna Brazell
'A Practical Guide to Secondary Liability and Joint Enterprise Post-Jogee' by Joanne Cecil & James Mehigan

'A Practical Guide to the Pre-Action RTA Claims Protocol for Personal Injury Lawyers' by Antonia Ford
'A Practical Guide to Neighbour Disputes and the Law' by Alexander Walsh
'A Practical Guide to Coercive Control for Legal Practitioners and Victims' by Rachel Horman
'A Practical Guide to the Law of Driverless Cars – Second Edition'
by Alex Glassbrook, Emma Northey & Scarlett Milligan
'A Practical Guide to TOLATA Claims' by Greg Williams
'A Practical Guide to Elderly Law – Second Edition' by Justin Patten
'A Practical Guide to Responding to Housing Disrepair and Unfitness Claims' by Iain Wightwick
'A Practical Guide to the Law of Bullying and Harassment in the Workplace' by Philip Hyland
'How to Be a Freelance Solicitor: A Practical Guide to the SRA-Regulated Freelance Solicitor Model' by Paul Bennett
'A Practical Guide to Prison Injury Claims' by Malcolm Johnson
'A Practical Guide to Advising Clients at the Police Station' by Colin Stephen McKeown-Beaumont
'A Practical Guide to Antisocial Behaviour Injunctions – Second Edition' by Iain Wightwick
'Practical Mediation: A Guide for Mediators, Advocates, Advisers, Lawyers, and Students in Civil, Commercial, Business, Property, Workplace, and Employment Cases' by Jonathan Dingle with John Sephton
'The Mini-Pupillage Workbook' by David Boyle
'A Practical Guide to Crofting Law' by Brian Inkster
'A Practical Guide to the Law of Domain Names and Cybersquatting' by Andrew Clemson
'A Practical Guide to the Law of Gender Pay Gap Reporting' by Harini Iyengar
'NHS Whistleblowing and the Law' by Joseph England
'Employment Law and the Gig Economy' by Nigel Mackay & Annie Powell
'A Practical Guide to Noise Induced Hearing Loss (NIHL) Claims' by Andrew Mckie, Ian Skeate, Gareth McAloon
'An Introduction to Beauty Negligence Claims – A Practical Guide for the Personal Injury Practitioner' by Greg Almond
'Intercompany Agreements for Transfer Pricing Compliance' by Paul Sutton
'Zen and the Art of Mediation' by Martin Plowman
'A Practical Guide to Adoption for Family Lawyers' by Graham Pegg

'A Practical Guide to Industrial Disease Claims' by Andrew Mckie & Ian Skeate
'A Practical Guide to Conducting a Sheriff Court Proof' by Andrew Stevenson
'A Practical Guide to Vicarious Liability' by Mariel Irvine
'A Practical Guide to Applications for Landlord's Consent and Variation of Leases' by Mark Shelton
'A Practical Guide to Relief from Sanctions Post-Mitchell and Denton' by Peter Causton
'A Practical Guide to Equity Release for Advisors' by Paul Sams
'A Practical Guide to Financial Services Claims' by Chris Hegarty
'A Practical Guide to Financial Ombudsman Service Claims' by Adam Temple & Robert Scrivenor
'A Practical Guide to Running Housing Disrepair and Cavity Wall Claims – Second Edition' by Andrew Mckie & Ian Skeate
'A Practical Guide to Holiday Sickness Claims – Second Edition' by Andrew Mckie & Ian Skeate
'Arguments and Tactics for Personal Injury and Clinical Negligence Claims' by Dorian Williams
'A Practical Guide to Drone Law' by Rufus Ballaster, Andrew Firman, Eleanor Clot
'On Experts: CPR35 for Lawyers and Experts' by David Boyle
'An Introduction to Personal Injury Law' by David Boyle

www.ingramcontent.com/pod-product-compliance
Lightning Source LLC
LaVergne TN
LVHW022314200926
848481LV00004B/1343
* 9 7 8 1 9 1 6 6 9 8 7 1 0 *